Hello from Inside

Creating a Positive Experience

Gen Z

Hello From Inside
Copyright © 2021 by Gen z

All rights reserved. No part of this publication may be reproduced, distributed, or transmitted in any form or by any means, including photocopying, recording, or other electronic or mechanical methods, without the prior written permission of the author, except in the case of brief quotations embodied in critical reviews and certain other non-commercial uses permitted by copyright law.

Tellwell Talent
www.tellwell.ca

ISBN
978-0-2288-4572-0 (Hardcover)
978-0-2288-4571-3 (Paperback)

Hello from Inside

In 2020 it all began ... a pandemic that rocked the world from China, Egypt, Columbia, United States, New Zealand, France, and beyond.

Throughout the countries this virus spread creating panic as people talked on phones, watched TV, and shopped in stores. The fear of COVID-19 radiated in cities and communities.

The virus spread to more people every day. When moms, dads, and children left their houses they were expected to put on masks. The rules of separation, they had to obey.

They had to social distance, stand six feet apart. Everyone who shopped stood in a line outside the stores, while they disinfected the carts.

The leaders of the country were in great upheaval. Chaos filled the minds of the people.

"Let's stay inside. Let's shut the doors. Let's close the schools, churches, parks, and beaches. Everyone, stay inside and self-isolate." That was the message on the news.
"This is how to kill the bad bug that might get you," the people were told.

Parents, teachers, and leaders used video chats to encourage family members, students, and others to disinfect and quarantine and tell them where they could shop and hike.

Sweet grandparents were locked inside unable to be hugged. No one wanted to give them that nasty virus bug.

Animal and produce products were destroyed. Millions of gallons of milk were dumped down the drain. Food crops were plowed under or given for free to people in need. Restaurants and small businesses closed their doors. Everyday life was reinvented and new possibilities were explored.

News on the radio, TV, social media, and the like advertised shortages of toilet paper, hand sanitizer, food, and cleaning supplies.

Fires burned through millions of acres. Many homes, animals, and valuable items burned or were lost.

Offence was given and taken in every way; each story was different in the part each had to play.

Riots and protests raged through cities. Hospitals staff, emergency responders, essential workers, and police were kept busy.

Babies were born and people died; sicknesses happened and many had no one by their side.

The mask that each person was expected to wear covered up the human story of what was going on under there.

The eyes of children were all that could be seen: no smiles, no frowns, no whispered words of mischief, surprise, love, or glee.

When someone by chance took off their mask to say good morning and let out a great laugh, the people around took notice, you bet, to enjoy the moment or choose to fret.

Upon reading this, I hope you can see the blessings we have shared in the home of the brave and people who strive to be free.

Let's stand tall for what's right. Let's protect our nation, children, friendships, and relations.
Our country needs us to stand together, inspire, build up, and protect each other.

Next time we stand by someone, remember, we don't have a clue what they are going through.
An encouraging word or act of kindness builds up and creates friendship and fondness.

These actions affect our day or week, so let's decide what kind of future we seek.
With the face behind a mask, it's hard to tell if someone needs help, encouragement, a laugh or simply a smile.

It's time we build a better future for ourselves and each other.

Protect our children.

This book is dedicated to all the children of the pandemic. It is my hope we can find something positive and upbeat in every situation. By pulling ourselves up and dusting ourselves off we can see how to make our lives better even when the circumstances aren't the best. This book is also a reminder to be grateful for what we have.

Thank you, teachers, doctors, firefighters, veterans, parents, patriots, and all service communities that think outside the box on how to best serve people in positive and effective ways.

Write your own 2020 story

www.ingramcontent.com/pod-product-compliance
Lightning Source LLC
LaVergne TN
LVHW051933070526
838200LV00077B/4636